Mother Want

Poems by Maria McLeod

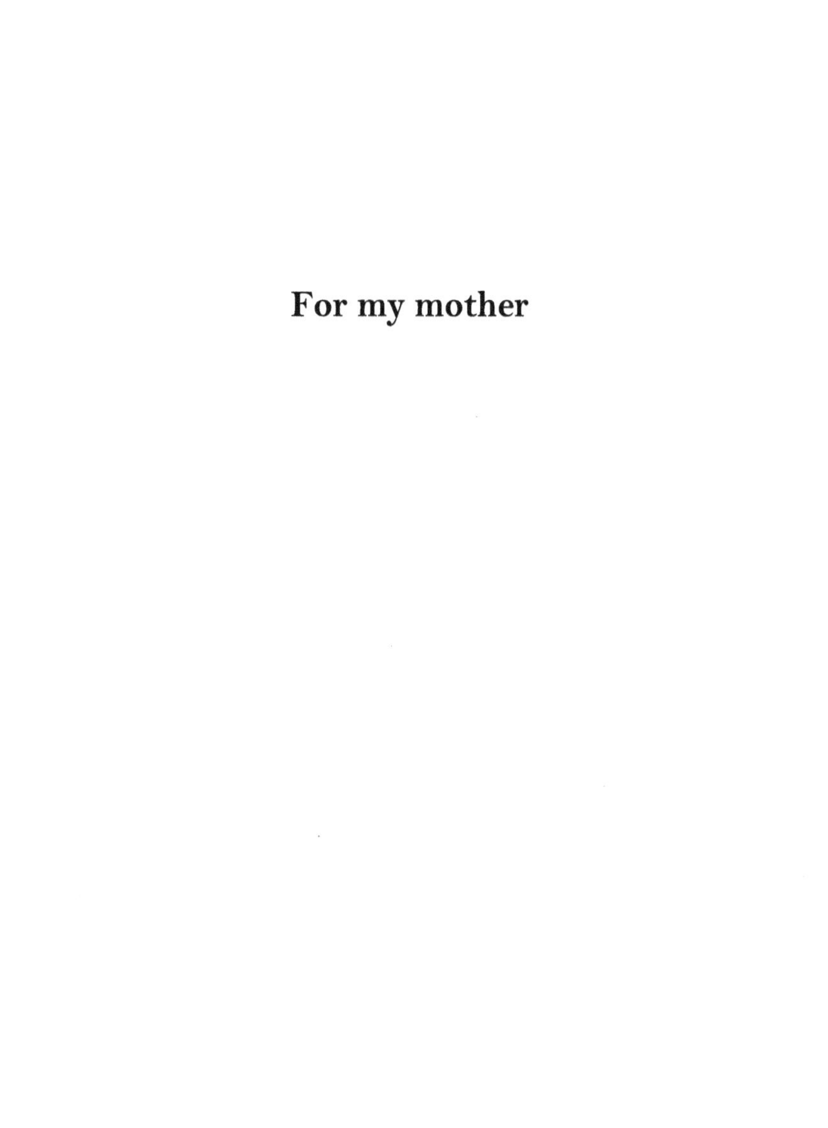

For my mother

Table of Contents

Mother Want

I want to be taken back
in, to be reintroduced,
starting with the inside,
to meet my mother
before the years of sleep:
days and days conked out on the couch.
I want to know her before she disappeared, before
she gave up being the mother, before she gave up
being the body of the mother, the breasts
and words and touch of the mother.
I want to get close, taste the meat
of her body fully open, finger the underside
of her ribs arched like church doors.
I want to love
what isn't lovable: tendons white
like crude electric circuitry; cartilage,
gristle of the bone; lungs stained brown.
I want to go back with the knowledge
of what I'm seeing, to decode her
like one would a cave wall.
I want to hear the words
that rattle in her throat
like birds caught in a chimney.
I want to empty her out, to ransack
her body, to cause damage. I want her
to shake off sleep.
I want her argument and her surrender.
I want her long hands, palms up,
where I can read them.

In the Woods Behind St. Mary's

Imagine you are 26, and someone has you by the wrists,
and your mother is on the other side of his closed office door
pleading, "Talk to him, talk to him,"
as if you've been brainwashed,
as if you've been caught stealing hosts,
which you intend to smuggle from St. Mary's
to a Satanic cult. Imagine
you are this 26-year-old woman whose only crime
is that she's finally refused
to go to church, and this priest has you
cornered in his office. Then he is chasing you,
as if you are the short-skirted secretary,
and he, the boss, going around and around the desk.
Imagine what you've done,
what you should have done
as early as eight years old
when your First Communion was really a mock wedding,
and you were required to be veiled and to wear a white dress
to walk up to the altar, a miniature bride,
with a groom-like boy in suit and tie, Stanley St. Claire,
who would, seven years later,
attempt to force you to perform fellatio
behind Mr. Linarski's garage. But this
is your First Communion, and you worry about biting
down on Jesus, fear dying
with his death on your conscience, and how long
would he stay there
on the roof of your tiny mouth?
Think of all those years in plaid skirts and anklets,
your father ordained a deacon, practicing
the benediction from the den,

the Gregorian chant
you still wake up hearing,
your mother taking home the vestments,
standing over the iron, and behind her is that picture of Jesus
knocking on the United Nations building, a palm leaf
between the frame and the wall. You, getting your ass paddled
for sticking that leaf down your brother's crack
one day when he bent over. Imagine finally refusing
because they're reading that Bible passage
about wives submitting
to their husbands.
And surely this is reason enough
for not going. Besides, you've been away
for what must be seven years now, and there's all you've learned
in your class on feminism and from that book
you're reading titled, *Eunuchs for the Kingdom of Heaven,*
not to mention those friends you have who are atheists
whom your parents blame for your moving away
and not marrying and not having children, something to show
for your life. Imagine this doughy-faced Father, this priest
in your face saying, "Let's talk about this
little misinterpretation of today's reading
that's keeping you away from God," his fingers digging
into your wrist, and the crucifix on the wall shows Jesus
bleeding from the ribs and at the places
where the crown of thorns pierced
into his head, while the miniature pope-in-the-glass
paperweight lifts up his hands, holy
as this body just inches from your body,
your voice repeating, "NO," and, "NO," and "NO,"
and "GET OFF ME,"
and you run for the door, and he's yelling
"Don't run, don't…"
but you do, using the shortcut
through the woods that are behind St. Mary's,

looking back to see he's not coming after you still,
so you slow to a walk,
and then you remember
how small you were
and how many years it is has been
since you've taken this path
to your parents' house.

Fidelity

for Emily Cora Penn

Today it is your cigarette
I remember, snuffed out
against the washbasin,
the butt pushed into the gouge,
the secret gap in the cellar's cinderblock.
You telling me, "Hush,
your grandfather is coming,
and he can't know I was smoking."
I am five and waving the air with you,
our hands flapping like paper fans
at the ends of our spindle-thin arms.
The two of us among the cobwebs,
amidst his baby food jars filled with nails,
on the same shelf with your old, dashboard Virgin Mary.
The backs of his ankles appear
between the slats of the stairs, the backs
of his calves, then his entire slender
backside. As he makes his way
toward us, you place sheets,
one at a time, into the soapy water,
while I stand wide-eyed,
forming my first alliance.

Joyce, 1945

> *für meine Mutter*

I find you standing atop a stool, age five, ironing
your father's Sunday shirt,
pressing down with all your might
to smooth the long white arms, the folds
of the collar, around the shiny buttons
and across the vast expanse of the back.
How was it you did not burn
your small hands? It's these scenes
you keep repeating from your fading
memory, as if you want me, your daughter,
to carry them into the world you're leaving.

Your brother Raymond, beaten
at only two years old for continuing
to crawl rather than walk, as he had for Kay,
the orphaned teen your parents had taken in
to clean house and care for the lot of you.
Kay thought they'd be happy to hear
that little Ray had taken his first steps
that morning; instead, your parents grew indignant,
standing over him, demanding he get up and walk.
"Steh auf und geh, mach es!"
His inability to understand and comply
equaled disobedience. They stripped him
so he'd better feel the strikes of your father's belt.
When he finally stopped wailing, he slipped
into shock, a trembling toddler on the living room floor.
You crept up to the doorway, looking upon that scene,
and when I was finally old enough to hear of it
you said, "I didn't know about death,

I just thought that Ray would be no more."

As if that cruelty wasn't enough,
they sent away his older sibling, Tommy,
age four, the little brother you'd mothered
and shielded from your parents' wrath
when your own mother had given up
and your father couldn't bear to claim him
as his own. *Retarded* was a word you refused
to repeat. Tommy cried your name, "Joy-cee,
Joy-cee," as they carried him kicking and flailing
to the rumbling Ford that took him to the institution
where he would be beaten into submission,
endure shock therapy, the currents
that couldn't cure his slowness. He never stopped crying
for you, even at age 50, when, at last, we met.
He looked past me to you, jumping up, clapping,
"Joy-cee!" Institutionalized all those years, he'd grown
stooped, malnourished, missing teeth,
but they couldn't erase his boy memory
of his favorite sister. You looked away,
pained, becoming that girl again, 1945,
the war's end announced in city after city,
air-raid sirens signaling the news
as you walked home from school.
Fearing bombs were about to fall out of that Michigan sky,
you began to run from the grown-ups yelling from their windows,
their porches, pouring out of the shops and into the streets.
You ran past them, heart thumping, weaving
around them, unable to discern joy from terror,
needing to make it home where you feared the sky was falling.
Falling. As it always was.

On Sunday, Our Father

Funny man, he drove the car
without using his hands,
steering with his knees
against the wheel,
us kids laughing, a mix of fear
and delight. Jokester/Demon. He was pure
impulse. If he wanted to lift his five-year-old up
by the hair and slam him back down, break him
to bits, he did. That was *his*
kid. Our little lives shifted on his axis:
happiness flipped on its back was misery.
We could hear the anger in his walk
across the hardwood floor, hatred of his wife
hooked to her cigarette,
ashen grey, rooted
to the couch. He held his hatred
of her close to his heart, his mistake
in marrying the damage
of his father-in-law's fingerprints.

Once, he punched a hole
in our bedroom door.
My little brother and I, terrified,
having locked him out,
a defiance he would not allow.
If he was set on beating us,
by God, you let that man
in. One Sunday, he tried to strangle
his namesake. He was eight, my brother.
"Daddy don't, daddy don't," a fat
hand around his throat. I stopped him

with my scream. A moan, a rocking
forward and back in my room,
on my chenille bedspread,
far and away my child voice grew
into a howl that bored through walls.
My mother gone, a rare escape,
for groceries. And what did my father ask
of me, "Please don't tell her, please
don't tell." And when tears leaked
from his eyes and he admitted
his horror, I took his hand
and held it, sorry he couldn't
help his rage from roiling up
and spilling over.

He laughed
easily. He laughed at us and threw us up
into the air and helped us change
out of our footed pajamas. He warmed bottles
of milk while my mother sleepwalked through life.
He made us pizza for dinner;
he let us drink pop. We loved
our father. He chased us, brought us
glasses of water before bed, took
our temperatures. He worked
and went away and came back
and went away again. We never
knew what we'd be met with
when he entered the door,
the full weight of his body
coming down on the ball
of each heel.
We learned to steer clear
until he cooled off,
knowing he could turn

on a dime. We waited
for a sign it was safe
to come out.

Her Parents' House

She wants to protect herself
from recollection.
To think back is to enter her parents'
house, nothing left but a child's
cryptic script. Her mother's voice
is an apparition
she reads as warning
of her world without end, a loop
a daughter hopes to fall out of.
Refuge is a self
inserted inside a self, slick as the space
between two teeth. She allows herself
to linger. Even now,
when her palms want to lift
in praise of some small memory,
she keeps them still
beneath her, and the past shrinks
to another abstract sentence: the place
we keep returning to is the place
we've just left from. It's the punctuation
she'll end with: a period,
an exclamation point, a question mark.

Mad Woman

She walks through the city with her left eye
          tripled in size, and her occipital lobe buzzing.
She can see inside   every
          body. She sees inside the cops, their eyes
so like her father's, a wet brown that bleeds
                                        into the iris.
The woods are full
          of search dogs. A woman's voice
tells her to outrun them.
          In the rain, in the dark, she is pure
                         muscle, protected by an unknown
          Goddess. She makes the cops disappear
                    when she shuts her eyes and sees
that her hands
                    have grown claws, that hate
          has a smell to it.

Venison

There is no way to say this pretty. The men could take an animal
down, gut it, drag its limp body out of the woods, and skin it. But
the butchering, that was women's work. They wore the blood of
it. As they cut and sliced and sawed, the women quit their talk,
clamped cigarettes between their thinned lips. Smoky grimaces.
They looked like men — all shoulders and arms and heavy torsos,
leaning over a body they were intent on taking apart. Mother,
auntie, grandmother, butchering freshly gutted deer on the
kitchen table. The scent of venison filled the trailer, end to end:
wild, raw, faintly metallic. We wore it in our hair, on our clothes,
our skin, in the sheets. We slept with that deer's death. We ate of
its dense, dark red flesh all winter. We were poor. We kept
potatoes in a bucket in the back of the shed. If we had onions to
boil, we had ourselves a meal. My mother worked her jackknife, a
shiny blade encased in carved stag bone. She cut the shrapnel of
buckshot out of the meat. Plink, plink, plink of BBs spit into an
emptied candy tin. That knife is the one special thing she owned,
and she never let any of us kids have at it. When I left home, she
pressed it so hard into my palm, it made an imprint. She made it
mine, metal and bone.

And the Sky Bloomed Pink

I learned about love
when I worked with horses,
rising each morning
before sunrise
to walk a mile in the rain
to the stables
in my ill-fitting muck boots,
mud-caked raincoat
and bib overalls—my Northwest
winter wear. I was 42
and had worked
plenty of jobs that had
required high-heeled shoes
and pantyhose, matching lipstick
and an upbeat attitude,
but I would have walked
10 miles in a blizzard
to work with those 28 horses,
patiently waiting in their stalls
for their heaps of alfalfa, fresh water,
and precious half-buckets of oats.
While they ate, I shoveled
clumps of shit and piss-soaked
wood shavings
from under their hooves.
Then, when breakfast
was finished, I'd slip
on their halters and leads
and walk them out
to pasture, sometimes four
at once, as the sun rose

over the mountains
and the sky bloomed pink.
Sure, I was bitten once or twice, suffered
more than my share of electric
fence shocks, and there was the time
when Cheers, the retired racehorse
with dementia, reared up
and nearly killed me had I not
gotten out of the way
and escaped with a bruised
foot. But what I came back for
were those sweet moments
mucking stalls, alone
with the horses at first light.
Frenchie, the half-thoroughbred,
half-European warmblood,
would sneak up
behind me as I worked
and ever-so-gently drop his head
to rest on my shoulder,
breathing so evenly
I couldn't help but halt
my task and hold still
to take in the miracle of it,
thinking, this is the divine,
the seraphic, to be touched
like this, together breathing in
the damp morning
mist, as if we both knew
such a simple love, unencumbered
by the ugliness inflicted by the world,
was worth steadying ourselves for
and embracing the weight of it.

November Green
for Mary

Among the Western red cedars, Douglas firs,
hemlocks, alders, and sawtooth ferns,
you tell me about the wife of a friend
who you recently learned was dead, 13 months post diagnosis,
her cancer having metastasized, spread, stage 4.
I am 13 months post my own diagnosis, my radiated breast
now firmer, shrunken, the surgery scars still evident: pucker
and pink lines. The drug I've been told to take
for the next five years to keep the cancer at bay
causes me to be cranky, forgetful, and subject to night sweats.
As devastating as it is to hear of another woman's demise,
I'm reluctant to refer to myself as *lucky.*
We reach a stone bench, marking the midway point
on our hilly hike through the forest.
We sit, two women talking of our work
as professors, of love and marriage, illness, and our parents'
decline. You pull out your cellphone to show me photos
of your 10-year-old daughter's hamster funeral,
how her friends arrived wearing black, some of the girls
wearing fascinators, as if attending a British wedding.
The hamster, Creampuff, is laid to rest in a customized
cardboard box buried in the black earth
amidst a spray of golden ginkgo leaves and sunflower seeds
the girls have placed there. You tell
how you explained decomposition
to your daughter who has marked her pet's grave
with a rock upon which she's written,
"Creampuff, the greatest hamster who has ever lived."
You want her to understand how the body will break down
and enrich the earth — that her pet's death

will generate new life.
We get up and keep walking, admitting to each other
we no longer know where we are, but trusting
the trail we're on will take us back
to where we started. It is a rainy late fall day, nearly winter,
and these woods smell of wet and rotting things.
Our trail is strewn with a thick carpet of dead leaves.
You note how interesting the colors, not so much orange
or yellow or brown. "Look," you say, pointing down the path,
"Look how these leaves have held their green."

Poem for My High School Graduation Photo

That crucifix you're wearing, the one you think is timeless,
will come off between Simone de Beauvoir
and Jean-Paul Sartre. At a point between undergrad
and grad school, you'll declare yourself an atheist
and then wonder what took you so long
to leave the patriarchal horror of Catholicism.
As for that V-neck green sweater, you'll hang on
to that. It's wool and you'll love green forever.
You'll grow breasts someday, and it will look
even better. Those braces you're trying to hide
behind that closed-lip, half smile
are going to come off, eventually, while
you pay for them in fifty-dollar increments
from late-night babysitting gigs and $3.10
an hour you earn as a cashier selling cigarettes
and lottery tickets. But you were right to want to beat back
those buck teeth. So much of your life will be about that mouth.
You'll get those braces off, and the pleasure of a metal-free kiss
will be your new-found freedom. You'll be amazed
by the smoothness of your teeth, your overbite now disappeared,
a smile you no longer consider hick-girl hideous.
You wanted a look that would last, having studied
the high school graduation photos
on display across from the principal's office, those generations
that came before you. How funny to find your father
there, his greased-back hair and skinny tie, the women
with cat-eyed glasses and bouffant hairdos.
You tried to keep it simple: a plain wool sweater, a crucifix.
It's your hair, that feathered look, that has a date stamp.
That's going to expire, along with your innocence, your wide-
eyed virgin self. Your pose is old school, too, the angle

of your head, and that backdrop — no one goes
to the photographer's studio anymore.
Now, you'd get your picture taken
in a field, a barn, a muddy creek bed, feigning a relationship
with the natural world. What are you feigning?
To appear already adult, not like a kid
with braces, a teen. Oh, how you wanted
future generations to see you as sophisticated, chic,
not confined to a bygone era, eternally out of it.
But who else were you attempting to impress,
who made you want to appear pretty?
An idea of a boyfriend, the guy you'd met
who worked at the petro plant across the river,
the one who took you down Canadian country roads
on the back of his motorcycle, all that wind
whipping your hair. You had no idea
what was coming. You barely knew
where you were — in Sarnia, somewhere
near the mouth of Lake Huron.
You'd yet to make your mark
on the world, more like a scratch,
just a young woman, waiting for the snap
of the camera's shutter, determined
to outlast yourself. Your *smile pretty* pose
held for eternity in a split-second
flash of light.

Hammer and Nails

The paint-speckled skin.
The tired, unshaven, uncombed,
unkempt whole of him. Sawdust
in his hair, the taste of it
in his mouth, bitter, hard to swallow, all these years:
hammer and nails, boards and pipes, bricks
and tiles, miles and miles of countertop and caulk.
In the dim, in the light, he surveys the hovel,
once another's home. He takes down walls, carries out
rotted wood, worn wiring. Echo of a woman
at the stove, the distant din
of a television, shadow husband
at the top of the stairs. He imagines where
he'll frame out windows, add a door.
Ghost voices in an abandoned
house. He's late for dinner, again,
time to pack up his tools, head home,
meet his kids' expectant faces,
the hard look of his wife. Just a little longer.
He measures his next day's work, makes his way
onto the dilapidated porch, faded color
he'll need to scrape off, recoat. Make it new;
make it right.

Death Defied

Somewhere my father is dying
his slow death of solitaire
and terrible TV
and daily injuries — the slips and falls
and bad diagnosis after diagnosis
of what will surely end, if not his life
then an element of it, like when he tried
and tried to ride a bike again
after heart surgery, but couldn't
find his balance and flew, head-long,
at 79, into parked cars and curbs
and over the neighbors' carefully manicured lawns.
He didn't give up until he cracked his head
in a stranger's driveway. Two days later,
my father returned in his car
to replenish the man's supply of Band-Aids
and gauze, telling him, "My gosh, I feel so dumb."
My father, who, as a sickly boy with rheumatic fever
and a damaged heart, overheard the doctor
tell his mother he wouldn't live
past the age of 12. He spent the school year confined
to his bed, Michigan afternoons with Soupy Sales
on TV, waiting for his classmates' well wishes,
small gifts: decks of cards, puzzles, comic books
and, once in a while, a sweet treat.
But at the end of that year he was supposed to die,
he rose out of bed, defying his doctors.
Making his way back to life, he mounted
his bike, pedaled down the River Road
past where he'd first caught perch,
his dad showing him how to thread

a worm onto a hook. He kept on, pumping
his once-weakened legs, pushing hard
against the pedals, past
the stretch of Saint Clair River
where his older brother had taught him
to waterski, to keep his tips up
lest he be thrown into the wake.
Bent over his handlebars, shirttail flapping
as if he might take flight, he passed
Diamond Crystal with its noon whistle
that could be heard across town, the men
knocking off for lunch, heading out
from the salt mine's dark depths, dusty white
from their work, like ghosts, lunch pails in hand,
looking up to see a boy on a bicycle zipping by,
"By God," they'd say, "death couldn't catch that kid,"
knowing nothing of how it had tried.

Letter From Pittsburgh

My window is at half-mast as the night breeze
ushers in a letter telling
of a friend's suicide. I unfold
the enclosed with one hand
over my mouth — one of the living
taking in the news of death, afraid
to inhale it. "Man leaps
from Panther Hollow Bridge,"
followed by text in past tense, words
void of flesh.

It is a marriage of two moments: his
life/his death. I'm left
holding fractions of both, traversing
the time-lapse as past and present collapse.

At summer's end, hollow
offers itself up like a hole in the heart
cleaved from a city by split rivers, held together
by steel, and now, this sound:
my friend, falling, like scissors
cutting through hair, through cloth,
as the ground rises up to meet him.

Bereft

for Stephen

By the time you hit the floor,
you've already fallen
into the arms of your father,
your young father, alive and strong and still able
to be your father.
Two days after his death
you're met by your primordial self, collapsed
upon the stone floor where you beat your fists
and cry "Daddy, Daddy" as if you've arrived at the door
of his death, and you want him to let you in.
Death has no dominion over your child self,
grieving not for the absence
of the frail father, but for the familiar
comfort of the sturdy back you mounted
before you could swim. Your small arms wrapped around his neck
as he broke the water's surface, holding you afloat;
the steadfast father, running alongside you, his teenage son,
race numbers pinned to your chests. Twinned.
You grieve not for the father whose booming voice shrank
to a whisper in his final days,
but for your unfailing professor father,
whom you, his professor son, follow
down university hallways
where students still call out his name,
your name, an echo lit
by window squares of light.

The Last Time I Saw My Mother

She is onion skin crisscrossed
with spider veins, cobwebs
of capillaries, a puzzle of bird bones
evident just beneath the skin.
The pulse at her wrist visible
like the beating heart of a reptile pinned,
awaiting the first cut, death
by dissection. My mother, my first body.
Her skin has drawn in
around the bones of her face, hollow
cheeked, false teeth slipping. Emaciated, gaunt
in the overly stuffed, upholstered easy chair,
curled up, fetal position, mouth agape, eyes
closed in this living room that smells of her past:
cigarettes and matted dogs, stained carpets
and an oily film across the walls layered with a coat of dust.
She's the skeletal body in the concentration camp photo,
a paleness the pallor of the open-casket dead.

My father and the hospice nurse try to rouse her —
"Our girl's come home to see you," my father says, voice cracking,
sentimental. "No," I say, "It's OK, let her sleep."
"Oh, but it's good for her to be awake," they say,
trying to un-crumple her collapsed body, trying
to push her up straight. What
have I come for? Her fingernails are adorned
with the outcome of a trip to a strip mall nail salon:
black and gold, with glued-on rhinestones,
all except for the nail of one thumb,
which is yellowed and pitted. It's evidence
of the new girl, her latest aide, the one who calls my forever

foul-mouthed, nicotine-stained mother, "Sweetie."
My mother, she would have hated her hands looking like that.
She would have squashed her cigarette butt in a tin lid
and cursed us, "God-damn-you-all," for her hideous hand art.

Her eyes flutter open, her pupils are but pin holes, irises
turned from blue to gray. She's like a leaf, fallen
from its tree, losing its color, drying out.
She doesn't see me. Her eyes don't move, don't settle upon me.
Her voice is a mumble, a series of slurry words, small cries,
but she's talking to ghosts, all the dead who have gone before her.
"Tell her you're here," someone says. "Give her a hug,"
someone else says. "No," I say, "I don't think so."
She never liked to be touched, nor to touch
or hold others. She went stiff at the very idea
of an embrace. Still, I try, I take her hand,
"Momma," I say. "Momma?" She feels unexpectedly
warm. I try to recall being small, try to block out
the expectant faces of the audience around me. "I'm here,
Momma?" The words exit my mouth in odd angles, like a script
I've yet to memorize, a school play in which I've been forced
to take part. When did I last call her momma,
wasn't I just a child?

The aide enters the room with a bowl of pinkish liquid
and an oversized, blunt-edged syringe, no needle.
Tomato soup. She fills the syringe with it
and holds it to my mother's mouth.
She grasps my mother's face with one hand,
gently, syringe with the other. She's working
to get her to raise her chin, to turn up her face
so she can squirt the soup and have my mother take it in.
I watch this, the demonstration of meal time, the two ounces
they hope against hope she'll eat. Soup escapes her lips,
dribbles down the sides of her face.

She resembles a messy baby bird. She closes her eyes,
swallows, as her aide coos: "Good, honey,
sweetie, oh, that's good."

Found Harbor

Upon the mudflats, we breathe in the sweet stench, careful not to crush
the small skeletons scattered across the gleaming, belching surface — a battlefield
exposed by low tide.

The purple starfish, too dimwitted to realize it shouldn't have remained
in the diminishing shallows, is left to dry out in the midday sun, its arms gone stiff.

A heron, frozen on the verge of a kill, breaks the stillness — a quick stab
at a silver-skinned flash of light.

The tremendous swallow follows — a flipping and wriggly fish shot down
the prehistoric gullet of a bird whose legs its catch had confused for reeds.

What is left, what is left?

I knock on the shell of a boat that holds the shape of my father, and it spits out dust, knotted
debris, the slightest whiff of me. And my mother, Medusa of the cistern,
held upside down all those years under water, where, oh where, is she?

I never learned to love the scent of saltwater, but I am so much more buoyant here
than in the land of those lakes that bore me.

Boats return with the rising tide; seagulls circle over vessels rich with fish.
Fishermen dock and empty their nets, while the smallest casualties of the catch
are left glistening on deck: slim slivers of fish and one tiny, pink crab
grasping a wisp of seaweed in its claw like a broken tether.

Deadheading

We did not deadhead
the rhododendrons last summer,
and now, this spring, their dusty blackened flowers
crown the new green leaves, obscuring the flush
of fuchsia to emerge from hidden buds,
a disappointing pairing, when we could have,
with a little time and effort, made the return of their flowers
so much more lovely and unencumbered.
We didn't know then what we know now
of the body — how easily we falter
like leaves on the forest floor
I confused for lace
not realizing such delicacy
was due to decomposition.
It's a path unwittingly taken
toward departure, a slow, cellular
sloughing, a loss not realized
until someone
calls it up onscreen
and points to what's gone
awry. This is how death becomes you
before you're ready to give in to it.
Like dried flowers dropped into bath water,
you wear its tired beauty
as you sink
into the porcelain, petals
clinging to your hair.

Summer's End, Dogs

The golden retriever that smells of stagnant pond
and cattails woofs from a fenced-in yard. Steady, staccato, hollow.
From a daylight basement, a schnauzer yelps, frantic,
scratching the surface of a sliding glass door
while the mutt that spent her summer digging
and re-digging holes gives up her task to whimper
at the edge of a patchy lawn.

The children walked out in the morning mist,
oversized backpacks sagging as they made their way —
a crayon-colored army — to gather and wait
for their yellow bus to appear,
a door to open and take them in. Then,
a curb, a tree losing its leaves, a forgotten lunch.

A dissonant chorus of barks, and yelps and cries
of abandonment rises in crescendo.
The Rottweiler-pit bull mix paces the deck
of its hillside home, whining as if injured,
as if nursing a terrible wound.

I kneel next to the raised bed, ripping out weeds,
grasping the last strands of summer, the pock-marked
plum tomatoes and the yellow squash sure to fall
victim to an oncoming surge of slugs. It's all I can do
to shut out the unrelenting loneliness
of neighborhood dogs, announcing over and over:
someone is missing; someone is gone.

Gratitude

Thank you to my posse of poem fixers, proofreaders, editors and collaborators. This includes Marilyn Annucci, Carolyn Dale, Gwen Ebert, Steve Hughes, Nancy Keene, Judy Kleinberg, Pam Kuntz, Nancy Pagh, Caitlin Thomson, Carroll Ann Susco, Kellie Wells, and the team at Writers Relief who helped make this book possible. I am deeply honored and appreciative that Oregon State Poet Laureate Kim Stafford chose my chapbook as the winner of the 2020 WaterSedge Chapbook Contest, resulting in this publication. I am especially indebted to journalist and creative nonfiction writer Stephen S. Howie, my husband, who has heard every word of every draft, and is, somehow, always willing to hear more.

Maria McLeod, May 2021

Acknowledgments

The author expresses appreciation to the editors of the following publications where these works first appeared.

Mother Want – *Cream City Review*
In the Woods Behind Saint Mary's – *Pittsburgh Quarterly*
Fidelity – *Sister Song*
Her Parents' House (formerly "She Wants") – *99 Pine Street*
Mad Woman – *Arkana*
Venison – *Floating Bridge Review*
Letter from Pittsburgh – *Pittsburgh Quarterly*
The Last Time I Saw My Mother – *Off Menu Press*
Deadheading – *Apeiron Review*
Hammer and Nails – *Cirque Journal*